ALIVE AMONG DEAD STARS

A C CLARKE has published five full collections and six pamphlets, two of the latter, *Owersettin* and *Drochaid*, in collaboration. *A Natural Curiosity* was shortlisted for the Callum Macdonald Memorial Award. She was one of four winners in the Cinnamon Press 2017 pamphlet competition with *War Baby* and was commended in the 2005 National Poetry Competition, and longlisted in the same competition in 2014. She has twice won the Second Light long poem competition. She lives in Glasgow.

A C Clarke once again fuses poetry with speculative biography in her new collection Alive Among Dead Stars, in which she explores the birth of Dadaism and the Surrealist movement in a shattered Europe recovering from the First World War. Her vivid and adventurous poems immerse the reader in the cauldron of art, literature, and philosophy which transformed the Twentieth Century. Voices and forms shift and interact over a sequence of seventy poems, focusing on the love triangle between poet Paul Éluard, his first wife Gaia, and her second husband Salvador Dali. The poems are surreal, playful, conversational, experimental, and intellectual, painting a vibrant picture of remarkable people and times rich in creativity and intrigue.
— Andy Jackson

A delightful, though not unexpected surprise, A C Clarke's new work is true to form. A natural evolution from *Wedding Grief*, *Alive Among Dead Stars* is both familiar and intimately different. Just as it echoes the past, readers can see resonances with Clarke's previous work, resonating anew with further growth and skill. Dynamic, engaging, and ever-changing, *Stars* continues Clarke's fantastic ability to explore history through liquid forms and voice, delving into the many intimate tragedies of post-world-war-Europe with a respect not often seen in writing or film. Succinct and lean, neither excessive nor starved, Clarke offers a rare treat - a completed, sublime collection worthy of any collection or library.
— James McLeish

How do you pin the extraordinary fluttering of the butterfly of Surrealism and Dadaism which emerged from the trenches, in order to understand the 'vast canvases cavorting' and the 'barbecue of dreams', in the lead-in to the Second World War? Anne Clarke's astonishing verse narrative examines historical sources, and employs the experimental techniques of the movements themselves. The exquisite corpse is gloriously there, and it is vivacious, whilst the imagined Ricky's commentary fixes the almost impossible whirl for the reader.

This is a remarkable book, which explodes with the people and the times when Dada emerged 'like a clown's car' in those most dangerous of times. It manages to be both scholarly and yet, it's also a page-turner, and it speaks to anyone fascinated by that period, but it also speaks to now.
— Beth McDonough

CONTENTS

ERASURE

COLLAGE

PARANOIA

Alive Among Dead Stars

A C Clarke

Broken Sleep Books

ISBN: 978-1-916938-63-2

The author has asserted their right to be identified as the author of this Work
in accordance with the Copyright, Designs and Patents Act 1988

Cover designed by Aaron Kent

Edited by Charley Barnes

Typeset by Aaron Kent

Broken Sleep Books Ltd
PO BOX 102
Llandysul
SA44 9BG

A whole world alive among dead stars
— Paul Éluard, *L'Amour, La Poésie*

Erasure

NEWSFLASH

August 22 1914 Battle of the Frontiers

27000 French passports
cancelled for good

~~The Treaty of~~ Versailles is ~~signed~~ in Paris

RUE ST VINCENT JANUARY 22 1920

Well Poppa, here I am in gay Paree
with my guidebook, my letters of introduction, my French-
English dictionary. I need to be close to the action
you said, so I got me this *garno* five floors up
on the Rue St Vincent in back of Sacré Coeur,
dirt cheap and a concierge with black front teeth
who smokes a pipe. I can't understand her French.

There's a nice little bar-tabac across the street
and les Halles down the road – the all-night café
serves breakfast. Guess I won't starve. Another thing,
it costs way less to live here than you thought.
Suits me. I get to come here, meet the big wheels,
all these invites and I don't pay a thing –
even Gitanes on the house once I wave your card
[don't you listen to their anti-bourgeois bullshit
says Poppa, they'll sell, they gotta live. Seems like he's right
though I kinda wish it weren't so].

Tomorrow I go to the Palais des Fêtes,
for that Dada matinée. [Poppa's idea.
Guy called Picabia – he showed in New York
and Poppa thinks he's the next thing.]
Keep your eye on the future, I know that's your maxim.
Buy cheap before their value rockets,
today's *enfant terrible* is tomorrow's genius,
just look at Monet. Let you know how it goes.

Ricky

PARIS SPEAKS 1

Dada burst onto my streets like a clown's car
doors dropping off, loud bangs. Like a child's scrawl
debunking an expensive wall.
Like noisy laughter.

Hausmann's boulevards were bouleversed.
Bombs could be understood. Bombshells,
lobbed at the bourgeoisie by rakehells
who never rehearsed

couldn't. People got over-excited.
The sans-culottes had been forgotten.
À bas les Dadaistes the hail of rotten
eggs hooted.

RUE ST VINCENT JANUARY 31 1920

That was some show, Poppa! I know you said
Dada's hot just now so I thought there'd be crowds –
there were! Some looked like they'd come in off the street
just to keep warm. The first bit was dullish.
Tuneless music, incomprehensible poems
hissed through masks. A few people
walked out at this point. Then up gets a guy
with a weird accent – compared to his mine's Parisian –
and reads what I guess is a poem. I can't hear a word
because the Dada lot are ringing handbells,
swinging rattles. It's bedlam! And the audience
don't like it, start shouting. Far as I make out
it's something about *go back to Zurich.*
The guy's grinning, looks like the cat with the cream.

Next up this Picabia and his pal, André someone –
I recognise Picabia from the photos you showed me –
holding up a picture, doodle really. The audience
goes berserk. Not sure why. Picabia
hasn't finished. André fetches a blackboard.
Picabia chalks another doodle, André
rubs it out. You never heard such a racket.
Most everyone now is making for the door.

I seize my chance as the pair come off the stage,
'Pardon, Monsieur,' and hand him your card.
For a moment I think he's going to tear it up,
but he glances at it, says in English, 'I know him',

pockets it, turns on his heel. I've done my duty –
but what's the point? A guy who draws stuff to erase it
isn't looking for sales – though if anyone
could sell a rubbed out drawing it's you.
Just act like you believe I've heard you say
and you can flog any crap. I have a notion
these Dada folk don't *want* you to believe.
I don't get it. You remember Mike,
my old pal from school? I ran into him there,
been in Paris a year; should be good for contacts.
He's asked me along for the ride
when he drives out to Suresnes next week.

Ricky

SURESNES AMERICAN CEMETERY
109 Blvd Washington. Interred 1565, Missing 974

Missing in Action: kind way to say
rubbed out
not a single trace.

*

Paris streets slump at this hour.
There's little point in their trip.
Hillsides of white crosses have hijacked meaning.

RUE ST VINCENT FEBRUARY 7 1920

Can't say visiting graves is my idea
of a good time, Poppa, but Mike was dead set. Seems
some guy he knew, cousin or something,
could be buried there. This guy was picked
soon as they signed us Yanks up, raring to fight
says Mike, and after that no letters, nothing.
His family had guessed whatever the news
it wasn't good. Found out only last year
they were right. Mike had a notion
he'd be in this cemetery, other side
of Bois de Boulogne. Most all of the bodies
are Yanks from the Meuse Offensive. So off we drove.
He'd bought a wreath [God knows why – hadn't a notion
if Jim was even there, let alone how to find him
among 1000 graves.] It was nothing like
Père Lachaise, just rows and rows of crosses
for all the world like markers for planting out trees.
We must have been there a couple of hours or more
when Mike decided to call it a day. Laid the wreath
on the next grave he came to. [It started to rain.
We didn't speak the whole way home.]

Ricky

AFTER WORDS

Tarmac gleams under rain, a strip
of polished iron, a blade
in which you might catch the glimpse
of an enemy face. Don't ask
for directions. It's better not to know.

Gracious the tall poplars which lean
so near to each other, along the road south.
'We have seen too much,' they whisper,
'we will give nothing away.'
Silent the long fields. Which have suffered most.

on 18 February, Deschanel sent the usual presidential message to parliament. Deschanel ~~said that there was no higher destiny than that of serving France, and he~~ thanked the legislators for having permitted him to continue ~~to serve her in union with themselves.~~ He hoped to maintain ~~the national unity which had been so conspicuous during the war. "Our first duty is to define clearly~~ our diplomatic, military, economic, and financial policy ~~to the country. We can only build up our policy for the future on sound bases.~~ I appeal to ~~all the experience and talent of the members of this assembly on behalf of this act of sincerity and moral probity. To~~ strengthe~~n the unity between all peoples who fought for the right, and who, by reason of that fact, are great,~~ to strengthe~~n the bonds.~~

ERASURES

Dada
Nada
Dadada
Nanana
Da
Da

*

Gala ← ~~Helena~~
Paul ← ~~Eugène~~
Éluard ← ~~Grindel~~
Tristan ← ~~Samuel~~
Tzara ← ~~Rosenstock~~
Man ← ~~Emmanuel~~
Ray ← ~~Radnitsky~~
Nusch ← ~~Maria~~
Éluard ← ~~Benz~~
Rosa ← ~~Luise~~
Bonheur ← ~~Strauss-Ernst~~
Jimmy ← ~~Hans-Ulrich~~
Kiki ← ~~Alice~~
De Montparnasse ← ~~Prin~~

AFTER ÉLUARD 1

Gala and Paul and daughter and mother and mother and daughter
and daughter and mother and mother and daughter and daughter
and Paul and Gala and Gala and Paul and Paul and mother and
mother and Gala and Gala

RUE ST VINCENT APRIL 30 1920

You know what, Poppa, just as I thought I was getting
the hang of Dada, comes this Picabia show.
I went along – knew you'd have wanted me to.
Twenty-two pictures and no-one to see them but me.
One or two sale-stickers. Found out later
he'd sold to his Dada friends. Nobody else.
Say one thing,
couldn't be more in the spirit of Dada
if he'd been trying. That's what I don't get, Poppa.
Dada's all against art and dealers, right?
Why have a show then? Why sell, let alone buy?
And listen to this: that André I told you about,
Picabia's pal, turns out he had quite a collection,
Marie Laurencin, Modigliani, Derain.
Well the other day a dame he's been cheating on
comes into his rooms while he's out –
don't ask me how she got in – only takes a match,
incinerates the lot! Seems she left him a Dada poem
on top of the ashes. And you know what, Poppa,
I think *she's* got the hang of it.

Ricky

NEWSFLASH

May 16 1920 Joan of Arc canonised

France's fighting spirit sanctified
in a flurry of Latin. Just the tonic
after the unholiest of wars.

Deschanel train fell out of a President window out of a Deschanel
fell train of a President a train window fell out of President
Deschanel window of Deschanel train out fell a President

RUE ST VINCENT MAY 29 1920

Don't just keep up with the trends you say, Poppa,
Keep one step ahead – so I got me down to the latest
Dada shenanigans a few days back
[boy, I wish I hadn't], got smacked in the eye by a beefsteak –
and I wasn't even on stage! Should have left in the interval,
Picabia did, guess he knew what was coming.
First up what they call 'music'. One of the pieces
was three notes over and over, the rest just so much noise.
Next up a poet guy – didn't catch his name –
rolls in – and I mean rolls in! – stashed in a cardboard tube.
Declaims gibberish about chamber-pots.
And a guy blacked-up like a minstrel sticks a pin
in a balloon with Cocteau's name on it.
They've a thing for balloons, used two on the stage as balls –
and I don't mean balls you play with – for an 'artwork'
supposed to be 'the sex of Dada' (hell!). By now
the audience is seething. They start to sing
one of the old war ditties – the kind soldiers
sang on the march. My ears are hurting.
People are going out, not just Picabia.

But half of them come back for the next instalment
loaded with steaks, tomatoes, eggs. The Dada people
carry on. The poet reappears
in a yellow dress and a blond wig. Declaims
more gibberish. A fight breaks out. Another poet
leaps on the stage shouting *Vive la France
et pommes frites!* The organ strikes up a fox-trot
but you can't hear it through all the hullaballoo.

It's raining foodstuff, everyone gets spattered
including the salon owners. That's when the steak hits me.
I know they say steak's good for a shiner, Poppa,
but not when it's hurled like a baseball. I've had enough,
don't stay for the grand finale, the 'Vaseline symphony'.
Next day the papers are full of it, the usual
'is it art or isn't it?' boloney. You got to admit
these Dada guys sure know how to hog the limelight.

Ricky

The defeat of the Socialists at the general election of 1919 appeared to have caused that party to ~~be~~come ~~more extreme in its views. And after much discussion throughout the year 1920, a great Socialist conference held at Tours in December voted by a large majority in favour of adhesion to the so-called Third International, the international organization of Socialists which was~~ under the control of the Bolsheviks ~~of Moscow.~~

November 11 1920

THE COFFIN OF THE UNKNOWN SOLDIER BROUGHT TO PARIS

His star was doused, one among millions.
'I am Mother of my soldiers', says France
as clamour grows. This coffin
laid in a chapel's pomp and circumstance
far from the smell of cordite and gangrene,
under the arch which celebrates killing,
answers her needs.

The moment he's chosen
he becomes myth, this young man joshed
by his mates from the village as they slogged
to the battle lines, his sweetheart's photo
tucked in the pocket of his soldier's jacket
just where a bayonet might strike.

Collage

JANUARY 28 1921 THE COFFIN OF THE UNKNOWN SOLDIER INTERRED UNDER THE ARC DE TRIOMPHE

The allied governments concur
Germany must pay dearly
for losses she's inflicted;
the unknown hero
stands for a generation
sacrificed.

Abraham and Isaac aren't in their minds
when floral tributes bomb
into the trench dug
for his bones.

LOOKING FORWARD

That year the mornings wore the drab of asphalt
levelled over corpses, the skies of Europe
hung in deep folds as if they could drop snow
on you and you and you

yet also

in hidden valleys frost spun lace across
burgeoning trees.

RUE ST VINCENT MAY 5 1921

There's a new Dada show in town, Poppa –
artist's a Boche and no-one's met him
account of he's an enemy alien.
Did I say artist? At least the rest can draw.
All this one does is cut things up, stick them together
higgledy-piggledy. Not that I got much chance
to look at them properly. Trust Dadaists for that!

Just like a pack of school-kids horsing around.
Starts with a hullaballoo – one miaowing,
that André crunching matches. Half the evening
one of them runs about knocking into people.
To crown it the lights go out and they hand us
orangeade. It's a warm evening
so most of us down it in one. Then the guy
who was running about stands still for a minute –
he's the one with the funny accent, name of Tzara –
and tells us – no shit – he's poisoned one of the drinks!

I can take a joke as well as the next man, Poppa,
but that's not funny. I've had it with Dada.

Ricky

MAX ERNST

More like an athlete than an artist
more like an artist than his painter father
who axed the tree he'd left out of the picture
sooner than own to less than truth to life.

PARIS SPEAKS 2

My newest citizen, fresh-forged,
adopts my name. Monsieur Paris
le Taciturne does not betray
his origins, submerged

in a gimcrack workshop down Rue de Bretagne,
hunched over a table where
he polishes glass tourist ware
vast canvases cavorting in his brain.

AFTER ÉLUARD 2

Gala and Paul and Paul and Gala and Gala and Paul and Paul and
Gala and Gala and Paul and Max and Gala and Gala and Max and
Paul and Paul and Gala and Gala and Gala and Max

ÉLUARD DISPLACED

The host deserts the premises each night
roaming the streets, smoking like a cancer,
a man without a star in the moonless dark.

FRACTURES

Alliances form, fracture and reform
across the continent, across the city,
street after street, house after house, room after room
Max, Paul, Gala permutate their loves
Tristan and Paul and André break, remake
their bonds, a slim volume of verse
has the words ripped out of its throat.

ANDRÉ PRONOUNCES

'Schoolboy sentiments written for shopgirls'

sentiments for written shopgirls shop for sentimental schoolgirls
boy writing shop for girlschools school for written sentiments
boygirls

COLLAGE 1

'the systematic exploitation of the accidentally or artificially
provoked encounter of two or more foreign realities on a seemingly
incongruous level – and the spark of poetry that leaps across the gap
as these two realities are brought together.'

the systematic exploitation of the spark of poetry that accidentally
encounters a seemingly incongruous gap across foreign realities
artificially provoked to leap together as these two are brought more

level and systematic encounters provoke two or more foreign sparks
to exploitation of the gap across artificial accidents a seemingly

incongruous leap of realities that brought poetry systematically
incongruous to spark by accident foreign encounters that provoked
two or more to leap across the exploitation of artifice seemingly real
to level the gap

COLLAGE 2

Take a pair of sharp scissors. Cut out
an emerald butterfly, a paintbrush,
a mouth open to love-exploring tongues.
Stick them at random on a primed canvas,
paint over the cracks and hear
the ancient verities dissolve in laughter.
Meantime a poet with liquor breath
interrogates the night, a morning child
sits solemnly before her cup of milk
watching a barbecue of dreams.

PARIS SPEAKS 3

They congregate in my amusement parks
taking play seriously
as if fairground rides could be the key.
What larks!

They could be at a conference
for clowns, sad clowns –
most of them wearing frowns.
Where's the insouciance?

SURREAL PHOTOGRAPH

If you move the photograph a group moves into the sun if the sun photographs your moves the group goes in if the group goes into the sun the photograph moves

*

Eternity tantalises. These wicked whispers
throw curveballs
from star to star.

A 'beautiful picture'.
Time to evacuate.

RUE ST VINCENT 11 NOVEMBER 1922

Got me a new friend, Poppa – René,
who's in with the Breton crowd, knows the whole scene,
took me to meet the top guns for an evening
he said I'd remember. You'll never guess what –
only a séance! Not like the ones you've heard of
all mediums and ectoplasm, no sir!

These guys aren't into raising the dead.
Boy was it weird! I'm telling you, Poppa.
They put themselves to sleep – well some of them do –
and the ones still awake ask questions
not about buried grannies and such,
about each other. It's a wonder
they don't come to blows. It's not for me, Poppa –

why I'm telling you is that Boche artist,
the one you asked me to keep an eye out for,
is living in this poet's house out in the sticks –
sleeping with the poet's wife, name of Gala
says René and *she's* a dame and a half.
René's wangling me an invite –

there's a kid there so none of that Dada crap –
I'm curious to know what's going on,
René says this poet doesn't mind sharing,
believe that when I see it! Well, so long, Poppa,
I'll keep you posted.

Ricky

SÉANCE 1

'Q What will he [Ernst] do?
A *He will play with the mad.*

Q Will he be happy with the mad?
A *Ask that woman in blue.*

Q How do you see Éluard?
A *He is blue.*'

What will the mad do ask Ernst will that woman be happy see the
play what will Éluard ask how do you be happy with the woman
in blue who will play the mad ask Éluard is he the woman he's
blue

THE TAROT READER

Only her fingers speak as they turn
destiny on its back, lay out
the Wheel of Fortune, the Hanged Man.

The air thickens. Everyone round the table
leans forward,
spines turned question marks.

She sits back, folding her arms.
Her audience seems to suspend
breathing. Her lips utter strange accents.

Outside the heavy curtains Paris grumbles.
The clock beats like the thrum of her heart.

GALA'S EYES

Eyes 'black as currants'
eyes that track her lover round the room
eyes that give nothing away
eyes that reflect
the gazer back to himself
eyes that 'could pierce walls
pierce strong-boxes'
her future-grazing eyes

eye my portrait deaf man it will draw all the spaces without a
sound fill the silence only to make an exceptional change man my
spaces only change the portrait to make it without eyes deaf to all
sound except silence make changes to the man without a portrait
draw only sound silence the deaf fill the eye with spaces

AFTER ÉLUARD 3

Incest, two brothers circle their soul-sister
in her dress green as a cypress
like wrestlers looking for a hold;

the sky releases seeds of hail
which catch themselves on stormy thorns
in spouts of tortured fish red sand

whirled up from desert acres, but look
to the left the green sprouting from deadened fields
and the woman there her young breasts illumined;

a shifting light glows her nipples
cluster of roses, colony of red beetles.

THE GOD OF SCISSORS

A sudden shadow falls across the paper
like a black song engulfing love
'un homme chante' and the poet becomes a guest
in his own book. Come boy, says the god of scissors
let me give you life. Snip, snip.
I can snip you away, if not today
on one of a million days.
Do you want that?
I can snip your whole world
into fragments.
Haven't you realised?

RUE ST VINCENT 18 NOVEMBER 1923

That poet who's sharing his wife with the Boche –
the one I wrote you about, Poppa –
has upped sticks to a new house (his father's loaded).
I was down there the other day with René.
It's the darndest thing. Most every wall and ceiling
covered in pictures – nursery and all
would you believe? Crazy pictures too,
they'd give me nightmares – their poor kid!
Not cut-ups either, painted straight onto the plaster.
What's crazier, half are the poet's wife
stark naked, one of them tall as the living-room,
her guts spilling out of her belly, the background
sort of a jungle. Craziest of all
the poet is showing them off like he thinks
they're masterpieces. God knows what the wife thinks.
She doesn't talk to strangers, just caught a glimpse.
She's tiny! And frizzy hair. Don't know
what they'd done with the kid. The Boche was there though
lounging about like a movie star. You'd think
he owned the place. So, Poppa, I've done my bit,
gave him your card. Couldn't say what he made of that,
though he hasn't a sou by all accounts,
ought to jump at any chance.

Ricky

MURALS

The guest may engulf the walls the ceilings
the bed: the others drown, tendrils of water
coiling about their mouths, sluicing them
to bone and gristle: 'I'd not have thought
the countryside concealed such horrors!'

SÉANCE 2

'Q Who is Max?

A *Deep sea diver and Spanish grammar*'

Dive into Max who is Spanish and deepen the sea's grammar who
is the grammarian diving deep and maximising the Spanish sea

PROGNOSTICATIONS

When he names the tune in their symphony
they taste small pleasures, when he names
each thread in their tapestry they suffocate
their doubts. The bones of their love
are showing through, tears seep from
their painted eyes, oil their intricate poses.
When he names Ernst he names Dalí's future.

During 1923, Germany was shaken by ~~adverse international developments and by~~ a dramatic further-deterioration in the economic climate: ~~the year was one of~~ crises.
1924 Death of Anatole France. André Breton, Louis Aragon and others publish 'Un Cadavre' attacking what he stood for.

EXQUISITE CORPSE

Exquisite the corpse
of the ancien régime
embalmed in a thousand libraries

waxwork and paint
glossing ugly bones
cosmetics of the canon

RUE ST VINCENT 6 JUNE 1924

Told you, Poppa, that poet out at Eaubonne
with the crazy set-up vamoosed – no kidding.
Just walked out of a cafe one evening
no-one knows where, though everyone's talking.
And now his wife – the Russian dame –
is flogging his pictures. Some collection!
De Chirico, Laurencin, Derain, Redon, Picasso
 – the Boche too. Lord knows what it's all about.
She's still with the Boche. Maybe she needs pin money.
Guess she couldn't sell without her husband's say-so.
Or is he dead and they're not telling? René doesn't think so.
Auction's next month at Drouot's. I got the catalogue.
Wire me the cash – I'll sure pick up a bargain.

PARALLELS

Five weeks the life of the mini-state
which strove to free itself into solvency
shake off the grip of occupation;

three years the Franco-German-Russian
alliance that ended on a packet-boat;

fifteen years before the marriage vows
finally shattered;

thirty-five years
the life of the Republic which fell
under the jackboot.

Paranoia

21 January 1924: Vladimir Ilyich Lenin dies. His funeral is (at) tended by around a million mourners. 26 February 1924 the trial of Adolf Hitler for the Beer Hall *Putsch* begins. On 15 October 1924 André Breton publishes the first (Sur)real(ist) Man(ifesto).

1924: Paul Éluard leaves suddenly for Indo-China and is later followed by Gala and Max Ernst. They (re)turn (with)out Max Ernst.

1925: Volume 1 of *Mein Kampf,* begun while Hitler was in prison for what he considered 'poli(e)tical (c)rimes' published. A second volume follows in 1926. The book will become a (best)-sell(er) in Nazi Germany. Max Ernst establishes a stud(io)at 22, Rue Tourlaque.

1927: Trotsky expelled from the Politburo. André Breton, Paul Éluard, Louis Aragon join the French Communist Party. Max Ernst m(h)arries Marie-Berthe Aurenche. The Third Nazi (P)arty Conference is held in Nuremberg.

1929: The Great Dep(Sup)ression begins with the (W)all Street Crash. First meeting of Gala *Éluard and Salvador* Dalí.

1930: Adolf Hitler is app(an)ointed Chancellor of (Ger)many. Dalí paints 'The Bl(s)eeding R(N)oses'.

Alexander Chayanov is arrested in the "Case of the Labour Peasant Party". The process is intended to be a show trial, but it falls apart. Nevertheless, at a secret trial in 1932 Chayanov will be sentenced to five years in Kazakhstan labour camps. The following year Dalí will paint Lenin in 'The Enigma of Will(iam) T(s)ell(f)'.

FREEDOM

Freedom, the watchword
to liberate art from its reason
workers from their shackles,

splashed out in paint, in ink,
in blood. Dream on
cries André with the rest. Make it all true

the Soviets admonish. Sign up!
Sign off! The shadow-boxing
of earnest minds far from the gulags.

The Yên Bái mutiny: troops of one garrison in Tonkin, mobilised by the Vietnamese Nationalist Party, kill their French officers, but are overwhelmed a day later and summarily executed. Ernst paints 'Lop-lop introduces Lop-lop'.1931 The Paris Colonial Exhibition (o)pen(n)s in Paris. The French government brings people from the colonies to Paris and has them create native arts and crafts and perform in grandly scaled reproductions of their native architectural styles such as huts or temples. France hopes the exhibition will paint its colonial empire in a bene(arti)ficial light, showing the mu/brut(u)al (ex)change of cultures and the bene(mis)fit of France's (ef)forts overseas.

EXPO

Here at the borders of the city's heart
for three francs a time view a three million pound

peepshow: reconstruction of jungle ruins
to match the show huts where selected families

enact a version of their culture to gratify
millions wandering in on tourist

afternoons, ticking their dutiful lists.
Craftwork for sale – own an indigenous carving!

One that survived the fire. Gawp at a woman
cooking up rice, safe for the moment.

No need to probe. The money's coming in.

Need to probe. The money's coming in.
A cooked-up story, safe for the unenquiring.

One that survived last year's bad news. A woman
for sale – own an indigenous pro!

Coolies side by side in the rubber plantations
dutifully sweltering for the greater good.

Spend an afternoon here
to satisfy your curiosity. Racism? Tick.

Colonial exploitation? Tick. This version of their culture
narrates a nation ruined to fetch

a tidy sum. Unreconstructed.

NEWSFLASH

A wave of repression follows the Yên Bái mutiny that takes hundreds of lives and sends thousands to prison camps.

Good how they spin their history.
My streets are named for fables.
Elysian fields for warmongers. Heads fell
in Place de la Concorde. Today

the citizens enjoy a holiday
in a mock temple where the Tricolore
raised in the courtyard semaphores
Liberté ... Egalité.

NEWSFLASH

1929 Breton publishes the second Surrealist Manifesto. This is countered by a second pamphlet titled 'Un Cadavre' attacking his position.

REQUISITE CORPSE

Requisite the corpse
of a rigid doctrine
entombed in precepts

under cover of freedom
irrational rationality
free play of shackles

SURREAL DISUNION

Although a special part of its function is to raise a flag of truce
on the roof, it examines with a critical eye
the phosphorescent door, impossible
to assign borrowed clothes to the negation
of an unrecognisable shape. The entire aim
is a fog to cut with a knife. The notion
that cynicism is not enough, our allegiance being
to dreamers at the point of departure
is no way to play on words. Most certainly
wrestlers benefit from training
in the possibility of a week of Tuesdays.
Under these circumstances the day of tears
is passed in playing up the contradictions
between the open palm and the cupped hand.
I do not believe the reason it is done
would invalidate a single word.
The loner at the feast has no intention
of granting elegance to the Freudian concept
of singing out of tune. Surrealism demands
you get into the envelope of the sky
without knowing how to swim.

RICKY T TO HIS SISTER 5 MARCH 1933 PARIS

Good to be back in Paris, Sis - my God it's changed.
Looked up my old pad in Rue St Vincent.
New concierge and they've put in a lift.
You see these new blocks, these HTMs
all over the place. More lines on the Metro.
But most of the clubs keep going. Spent a few nights
catching up with friends. The art scene's big here,
like I told you. Dada's old hat now.
Surrealism's still in – boy, aren't those dudes
stuffed shirts! Dada was *fun*.

Latest, that André guy (saw him at *Palais des Fêtes*
years ago) only calls a Tribunal
like he's a judge or something, summons Dalí
(the painter we've got our eye on) to answer the charges.
Hitler supporter they say. Anti-Lenin.
For sure he's no Bolshie. But a Nazi?
They say he stuck a thermometer in his mouth
all the time they were talking at him,
checked it every few minutes. People were laughing.
Not André though.
Upshot is they've expelled him –
Dalí that is. Don't see what difference it makes.
He'll go on painting the way he paints –
looks pretty damn surreal to me.

TRIBUNAL

Gala, dont le regard de rat traqué ...[Georges Hugnet]

Yet you walked in as if
you owned the place

took your seat
with the careless hauteur

of one used to deference.
It wasn't for you

to fight Dalí's ground.
They were the rats

cornered by sanctimony,
helpless before his fooling.

You watched his antics
not moving a muscle.

*

Trials were in fashion between Wars.
Expulsions too. Guilt presumed.
If not the prison cell the gulag
if not the gulag the assassin.
Softer weather on Paris streets
where a spoof gun fired a joke message.

NEWSFLASH

1933 Hitler becomes Dictator of Germany

'HITLERIEN'

The year of Hitler's apotheosis - Adolf
was gearing up for purges. Dalí's last show
at Colle. Lenin disguised as Tell was hung there.

Breton and friends went in to smash the painting.
It was too high for them. Hitler and friends
were whetting their long knives.

Dalí and fathers – he had a thing. Hitler
and Jews. Dalí willed paranoia
to set his mind free. Hitler willed paranoia

to take the German people captive.
Dalí loves Hitler chalked on his freakshow psyche
in schoolboy script. Hitler hates art

unless it paints the Aryan lie. Cruelty
ran through them both, a seam of bloodred ore.
Adolf loved dogs. Salvador took his code

from Sade. Ultimate sexual freedom.
Dalí was Lorca's lover once, it's said.
Gays ended up in concentration camps.

What image did they see, these two,
when they looked in the mirror
where right is left?

PORTRAITS

A woman melds into a standing horse
neighs through her dangling arm
at her inverted crutch her bush roars
grows into swishing marestail   three-way perspective
as tricksy as a fairground mirror   images   `
vanish resurface again vanish each almost
but never quite there   over all
the sullen light of heatwave

*

Again a woman   in St Sebastian pose
draping herself against a pillar ecstatic
nude   right leg bent back so the knee appears as
the end of a stump   orgasmic martyrdom
dreamfloats her streaming hair her rapt expression
upended to a heaven she alone sees   and she's proud
to turn full on to the voyeur her basket
of summer-blown roses trickling their crimson petals
down her thighs   her bush a study in red

*

Two cypress trees lean towards each other
like the praying couple in that other
Angelus, the woman about to smother
the man. From her barrow seat she looms
like a praying mantis. The cypress looms
against the last light in the glooms

of a December evening. A woman opens her mouth
like a jug. A woman tightens her mouth
like a padlock. The Angelus fields laid waste by drought.

RICKY T TO HIS SISTER 31 JANUARY 1935 NEW YORK

You ask me, Sis, about the Crosby ball.
Is it true about the Dalís? Did the wife
really wear a hat with a dead baby?
Guess so. A doll, at least, but pretty gruesome.
Looked like it was rotting. And get this –
a lobster (he's keen on lobsters)
pinching its head. She's some dame, this Gala.
A mother too – most mothers wouldn't wear
a dead baby. I know everyone's saying
they meant it for the Lindbergh kid. Why would they?
You have to see the guy's other stuff –
crazy or what? It's all sex and corpses
ants and lobsters and the Lord knows what.
I guess the wife just goes along with it –
they know what sells, those two.
Won't have hurt them
to be in all the papers. Won't hurt us
to look out for a canvas or two.
He's on the up.

15 June 1935 during the International Con(gress) of Writers
In Defence of C(V)ulture(s) organised by the Communist
Party, André (B)r(igh)eton publicly slaps the Soviet writer and
journalist, (I)li(y)a (Eh)r(en)bourg(eois), for insulting comments
about the Surrealists. The latter are then ex(re)pelled from(by)
the Congress. René Crevel's efforts to reconcile these (two f)
actions fail.

PARIS SPEAKS 5

Brawls on my streets.
When have there not been?
Brawls between
intransigencies. Mule meets

mule. Each digs his hooves in.
A glare, a slap. This passes
for argument among the moneyed classes
removes

the need for tedious debate.
My citizens prefer simplicity.
The gutted heart a casualty
rescued too late.

DEATH OF CREVEL 19 JUNE 1935

A 'hard woman', yet behind
the glitter of her eyes was read
the smudged text of grief.
What grounds

have those who in a glow
of righteousness
have spun her
into snake-haired witch?

From her tricky pack
she laid fates out
like a washed corpse
timed war to the minute

but René's death was twisted
into his father's noose
war inked
into the peace treaties.

For him his kitchen gas
was the solution.
For her and Dalí a shared
moment of tears.

RICKY T TO HIS SISTER 1 JULY 1936

A great show at the New Burlington – massive!
Bound to be stuff to look out for. We should have bought into
this market years ago, prices are rising, but still
there's bargains to be had. It's not just artworks –
it's lectures too. In French mostly.

You wouldn't believe the one I went to today.
Wouldn't have missed it for anything.
This Dalí guy stomps in
in full diving-gear, helmet and all,
two wolfhounds on a leash. What's that about?
He starts to speak but you can't hear a word.
Loudspeakers bellow a muffle.
Soon he starts to dance – leastways that's what it looks like.
We all think it's part of the act. He's waving his arms,
shouting God knows what.
Some-one catches on. Cue frantic struggles.

Not sure how it's done but they get the helmet open.
Collective sigh.
Then he goes on with the lecture
like nothing happened – he's using slides now
any which way – sideways, upside down -
n'importe! he cries gaily and on to the next.
What was the lecture about?
Now you're asking.

EXHIBITION

For him, Great Masturbator, his 'orgies',
orchestrated to the last perversity,
took hard work, like brushstrokes; to release
his jism, climax of creativity –
            wasn't frottage a surreal technique?

Of course he was getting old, Gala remote
in her castle but his onanistic freaks
went back long before that. When he donned
a diver's helmet for that London lecture
was it simply to cause a sensation? Was it even
a symbol? It left him gasping for breath,
and gets presented as a stunt too far.
The way I read it: with customary precision,
he staged, as so often, a little death.

NEWSFLASH

1936 The beginning of the Spanish Civil War.

DALÍ AND GUERNICA

Like a flight of carrion crows out of the east
the Heinkels flocked over Basque country.

The small town shuddered
under the drumbeat of their wings.

Picasso painted it in black, white, grey,
grisaille of washed-out, bankrupt ideologies

monotone iteration *kill kill kill*.
In the streets black roses flowered from wounds

the smoked-out sun faded on
ashheaps of grief

soldiers, houses, horses, children, women
all in a jumble

and years on in that cruel Spanish light –
light of the *corrida*, of the *auto da fé* –

glares the white-colonnaded
monument to murder.

Plain black the line ruled down the middle.
It's one side or the other.

He doesn't want to choose either.
He wants only his life at the end of a brush

the comfort of money.
They pin a label on him anyway.

All very well to sit at ease at table
raising his glass to the light, admiring

the clear, deep red of the vintage. Doesn't he know
he's drinking his country's blood?

BLOOD

Dalí signed many of his paintings Gala-Dalí 'since it is mostly with your blood, Gala, that I paint my paintings'.

Our veins perpetually tidal

the red sea surging

until

heart-stop

Life transmitted to life

through intricate tubing

or

stored in frozen amphorae

like Medea's witch-baths

to revive latter day Aesons

but alas

powerless

to reverse time

Blood

The feared outflow

between a woman's legs

one drop

can wither a flower

or a manhood

monthly pollution forbidden to cross

the temple threshold

even though in a goddess

whose womb weeps

purest ichor

Blood

the crimson of sunsets and gashes
life leaking through its thin wraps
slower than water

Blood

stain on the moon
presaging opening of veins
ink for the sealed oath
dye for murderous hands

NEWSFLASH

1939 Spanish Civil War ends with Nationalist victory. Francisco Franco becomes Spanish leader.

KRISTALLNACHT

A glass splinter in a cocktail
reddening with the drinker's blood.

Windows stove in. A synagogue in splinters.
Blood for blood.

A cut finger. Surreal dandy at the bar
dangling a false cherry

against the real thing. A shot
in an embassy a border

away. A bloodred cocktail
on a bar counter. Laughter

splintering the air. Crack
of breaking panes. 'Blood

sweeter than honey' cries
the selfmade madman bounding

goatlike into the air. Blood
asks for sweet revenge.

The artist leaps on an astonished tram.
Work-able Jews are herded onto

trains rolling towards the labour camps.
A splinter quivers in a sea of blood.

NEWSFLASH

1940 German forces occupy Paris.

PARIS SPEAKS 6

Since my beginning I have known turmoil,
soldiers' feet stamping my thoroughfares,
blood on my squares,
assorted rabble.

The Panzers filing past, slow as hearses,
endless corteges that marked my funeral –
these were different. In scale
but more, in kind. Worse

violence has racked me. Indeed
there was none. A cold power
dictated rules of war
must be obeyed

to the last umlaut. No question
either – the government thumbed down
to make what terms it could, and out of town –
who dictated rules of occupation.

NEWSFLASH

1940 Ernst, Dalí and Gala escape to America. 1941 Max Ernst marries Peggy Guggenheim in the US. Breton escapes to America. Paul and Nusch Éluard join the French resistance. 1941 Éluard's poem 'Freedom' dropped by RAF planes over France. 1943 Lou Strauss-Ernst, Ernst's first wife, is executed in Auschwitz.

THE LAST HURRAH OF THE SURREALISTS

sounds in the siren calling
for departure. On Paris streets

the lights go out early. This is the time
of lethal paperwork, the stitching
of yellow stars.

*

Europe abandoned, the smoke
of departing steamers a smear
on the Atlantic horizon.

Ernst burned his boats. Dalí
turned from the hollow face
of war, skulls within skulls,

the melting telephone,
the appeaser's
bat-umbrella blown outside-in

to the tranquil homage
of rich women
a free pass to celebrity.

*

The images are fading
outgunned by war.

Surrealism's Pope in exile
Lop-lop building his desert cabin

Avida chasing dollars while Gala
checkmates him at the chessboard.

The century's next half is loaded
into the projector ready to run.

p.20, Erasures: it is notable how many of the Dadaists and Surrealists adopted names different from their birth names.

p.21 and p.36, After Éluard 1, After Éluard 2: suggested by Éluard's poem *Berceuse* (*Les nécessités de la vie*, 1921). The text of Éluard's poems referred to is the definitive *Paul Éluard: Œuvres Complètes* Éditions Gallimard 1968, Tome I.

p.35, Paris Speaks 2: at the time when Max Ernst came to settle in France he was still classed as an enemy alien and he entered the country under a false passport in the name of Jean Paris. He was nicknamed 'le Taciturne' in the workshop where he found work for a time because he said so little (probably so as not to reveal his German accent).

p.39, André Pronounces: comment on Éluard's poems by André Breton, in a fit of pique, as quoted in *Gala: La Muse Rédoutable*, Dominique Bona, Flammarion 1995.

p.40, Collage 1: Max Ernst's definition of collage, unattributed internet translation.

p.43, Surreal photograph: the first stanza is a scrambled version of the author's translation of Éluard's poem *L'Ami* (*Les nécessités de la vie*, 1921)

p.45, 46, Séance 1, The Tarot reader: the dialogue is between Robert Desnos, as medium, and André Breton as interrogator, as quoted in *Gala: La Muse Rédoutable* (See above). Séances invoking not spirits but the unconscious were popular among the Surrealists during the 1920s. Gala was a noted reader of the Tarot pack.

p.48, Deaf Man's Eye: the first stanza is a scrambled version of the author's translation of Éluard's poem *Œil de Sourd (Répetitions,* 1922)

p.49, After Éluard 3: suggested by Éluard's poem *Max Ernst* (*Répetitions*, 1922)

p.50, The god of scissors: references *Les malheurs des immortels* (1922), a collaboration in which Éluard supplied the poems and Ernst the images, collages made from cut up photographs and drawings.

p.52, Murals: 'I'd not have thought/the countryside concealed such horrors!': André Breton's comments after a visit to Éluard's house at Eaubonne.

p.56, Exquisite Corpse: the name of the word-game invented by the Surrealists for the random generation of disparate images and ideas.

p.58, Parallels: the 'mini-state' is the Rhenish Republic, an attempt to establish the Rhineland, which bore the economic burden of the reparations imposed on Germany by the Treaty of Versailles, as a separate state.

p.71, Surreal Disunion: the poem splices extracts from the *Second Manifesto of Surrealism* in an unattributed translation published on the web-site of Maria Elena Buszek with excerpts from the author's translation of *Ralentir Travaux* (1930), a collaboration between Éluard, Breton and René Char.

p.76, Portraits: the first section refers to Salvador Dalí's painting *Sleeping woman, horse, lion* 1930; the second section to his *Bleeding Roses* 1930; the third to his *Archaeological Reminiscence of Millet's Angelus* 1933.

p.81, René Crevel committed suicide like his father before him. Dalí and Gala were close friends of Crevel.

p.90, Kristallnacht: Kristallnacht, 'Night of Broken Glass', took place in 1938 and was an organised attack on Jewish homes, shops, synagogues etc. The episode with the glass splinter is recounted by Dalí in his notoriously unreliable 'La Vie Secrète de Salvador Dalí.'

AFTERWORD AND ACKNOWLEDGEMENTS

This collection focuses on the emergence of Dadaism and Surrealism as experienced in Paris after World War One by the poet Paul Éluard, his first wife Gala, her second husband Salvador Dalí and their circle. Their complicated relationships parallel in many ways the alliances and divisions in Europe between the wars and the absurdist elements of Dada in particular were a direct response to the disillusionment with past tradition created by the senseless horrors of the First World War, in which several of the group had served at the Front.

The collection is deliberately fragmented, drawing on elements used by the Dadaists and Surrealists themselves, as referenced in the titles of the three sections, Erasure, Collage and Paranoia, including cut-up techniques, random word choice and so on. It was originally written as a series of texts mainly without title. Translations from the work of Éluard and others are incorporated into some of the poems and where that is the case it is acknowledged in the appended Notes, which have been kept to a minimum since enough context is provided, I hope, by the factual content of the collection itself. Ricky, the young son of an American art dealer, is a fictional figure created to provide an outsider's take on some of the more notable episodes in the development of Dada and Surrealism.

This book would never have come into being without the inspiring encouragement of Donny O'Rourke, to whom I am deeply indebted, as I am to Broken Sleep for taking me on and in particular to Charlotte Barnes for her meticulous editing. All errors in the work are my own.

Some of these poems have appeared in *Dreich* and *The Poet's Republic*.

LAY OUT YOUR UNREST

www.ingramcontent.com/pod-product-compliance
Lightning Source LLC
Chambersburg PA
CBHW030849090426
42737CB00009B/1156